IMAGES OF ENGLAND

THE CO-OP
IN BIRMINGHAM

IMAGES OF ENGLAND

THE CO-OP
IN BIRMINGHAM

LINDA AND ANTHONY CHEW

TEMPUS

Frontispiece: A 1940s wartime window display of 'POM' dried and tinned potato.

First published 2003

Tempus Publishing Limited
The Mill, Brimscombe Port,
Stroud, Gloucestershire, GL5 2QG

British Library Cataloguing in Publication Data.
A catalogue record for this book is available from the British Library.

ISBN 0 7524 3098 X

Typesetting and origination by Tempus Publishing Limited
Printed in Great Britain by Midway Colour Print, Wiltshire

Contents

Acknowledgements

We would like to thank local author Margaret Green for her invaluable help in compiling this book, particularly for assembling Chapter Six. Thanks also to John, Lyn and Rebecca in the Co-op Member Relations Office, Chris Shelley, Mark Hudson, other members of the Co-op History Group and finally to our son Duncan for his practical help, advice and support.

This book is based mainly on the photographic and other records of the publicity department of the former Birmingham Co-operative Society. Other material has been donated and added to the archives, for which Midlands Co-op is very grateful. The poster on page 102 was kindly lent by Birmingham Library Services and the TASCOS photographs in Chapter Seven are used with the permission of Birmingham Planning Department.

A somewhat bizarre photograph of the BCS president and his committee as they toured the Vauxhall Road Dairy in 1950.

Introduction

For generations of Birmingham folk, the 'Co-op' was more than a shop on the High Street, it was a way of life. At an early age, the children of co-operative families were taught to chant their mother's Co-op number. The dividend on purchases, (which could be up to 2s (10p) for every £1 spent), was eagerly awaited, and families could use it to buy new shoes or school uniforms for the children, winter coats, or other larger purchases. Yet, more than this, the Co-op offered people a sense of community and worth, whether through the Co-operative Women's Guilds, the educational and leisure activities run by the Society or at the members' meetings. The Co-op was owned by its members and was there for everyone.

This cornerstone of working-class life claims its origin from the endeavours of a group of Rochdale weavers who, in 1844, began trading goods on a co-operative basis. Though this was not a new idea, the Rochdale Pioneers, as they became known, offered a formula for co-operative trading that redistributed profits to its members, dealt in cash only and promoted democratic control in a time when few working men had the vote. The success of this one society led other groups of workers to band together and form consumer co-operative societies of their own. Around Birmingham, however, it was not until 1875 that co-operation could claim its first real success when, in the small village of Stirchley, the Ten Acres and Stirchley Street Co-operative Society Ltd was formed. This was followed, in 1881, by the Birmingham Industrial Co-operative Society Ltd, which had its origins amongst the railway workers of Saltley. Finally, in 1887, the Soho Co-operative Society Ltd was formed. These would eventually constitute the Birmingham Co-operative Society Ltd.

In the early days, co-operative societies were small, with a few hundred members, and their stores were often confined to the back streets. By 1900 the societies in Birmingham could count their membership in the thousands and moved from small corner shops, often converted from dwellings, to purpose-built stores. They developed a distinctive architecture, often with the logo of the Society proudly displayed on the pediments. This expansion reached its height with the building of new Central Premises, such as the Birmingham Co-operative Society's store in High Street, City Centre and the imposing TASCOS department store in Stirchley. These were grand affairs, often with oak-panelling, wrought-iron work and polished brass fittings. The Co-op had achieved great success and was proud to show it.

The ordinary members' enthusiasm for the Co-operative store was matched by their involvement in the activities of the Society. The Co-operative Women's Guild played an important part in promoting the Society and in raising social issues such as child welfare and women's health. The Co-op also organised educational classes for adults and children in a wide range of subjects, from Co-operative history to bookkeeping and accounting. Leisure activities such as dances, outings and sports were available to employees and members. All of these helped to create a Co-operative culture of caring and sharing.

The Co-op led the way in many areas of retailing and production. As early as 1908, the Birmingham Co-operative Society could boast the largest and most modern bakery in the city, while TASCOS was offering safe, hygienic milk from its model dairy in 1910. In the shops, the Co-op perfected methods of organisation, presentation and promotion that were far ahead of their time. From the 1920s, the Co-op was promoting trade with special offers and discount vouchers and, after the Second World War, was the first retailer in Birmingham to develop self-service.

While much has changed, the Co-op is still flourishing. It is unique among retailers in that surplus profits are not paid out to shareholders but are used to benefit its members and the community. The Co-op has pioneered ethical trading and is deeply committed to responsible retailing. It is attracting new members and maintaining the ideals laid down by its founders in Rochdale in 1844. Through merger activity, the Birmingham Society is now part of Midlands Co-operative Society Limited, a major regional society trading across six counties with a turnover in excess of £750 million. It is one of Britain's strongest consumer co-operatives with its sights firmly set on continued growth.

Anyone interested in joining the Midlands Co-operative Society Ltd, or requiring more information on its activities, should contact the Member Relations Office at the Birmingham & Midland Institute, Margaret Street, Birmingham B3 3BS.

ABBREVIATIONS USED IN THIS BOOK:

BCS   Birmingham Co-operative Society Limited
BICS   Birmingham Industrial Co-operative Society Limited
CWS   Co-operative Wholesale Society Limited
TASCOS   Ten Acres and Stirchley Co-operative Society Limited

BIBLIOGRAPHY:

75 Years of Co-operative Endeavour by Harry M. Vickrage
The Co-op in Birmingham & the Black Country by Ned Williams
History of the Birmingham Co-operative Society Limited 1881-1931
Seventy Years of Service by T. Smith
Souvenir of the Opening of New Central Premises
Your Voice and *Home* Magazines

Birmingham Central Library also has a vast archive of Co-operative material.

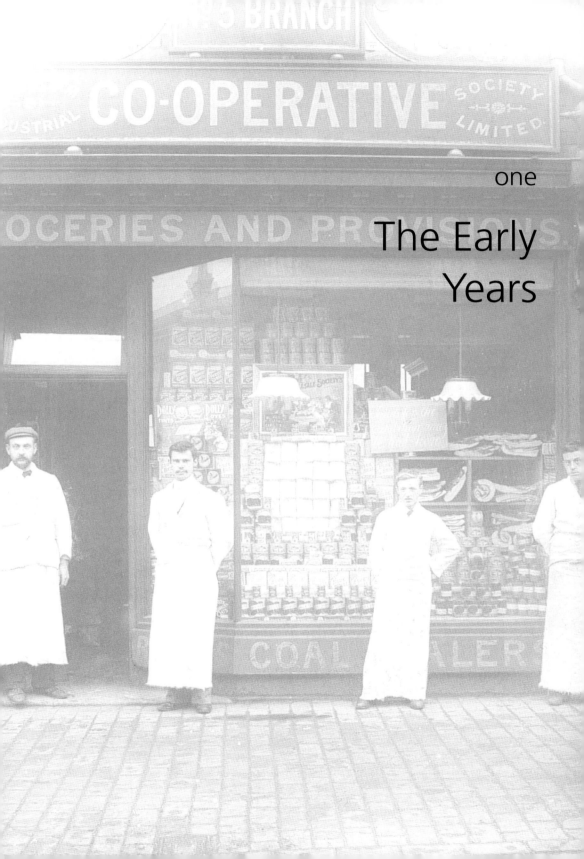

one

The Early
Years

The Birmingham Industrial Co-operative Society opened its first shop on Friday 5 August 1881 at 14 Great Francis Street. It was referred to as a 'small and unpretentious shop, characteristic of so many similar small shops to be found in working-class localities'. By 1884, larger premises were needed and the shop shown here, on the corner of Great Francis Street and Newdegate Street, was purchased.

This would become the Society's headquarters and Central Premises for the next thirty-two years. The Society immediately appreciated the value of good display as is demonstrated here.

Two excellent views of around 1931 of the shops, with extensions for boot repairs and stabling. Adjoining premises had been purchased, which gave provision on the first floor for a reading room, boardroom and offices.

The Central Premises were still proving to be inadequate and were disadvantaged by not being geographically centred. More office space was also needed and the obvious solution was to purchase property in the city centre (described in Chapter Two).

Above: Branch No. 1, 17 Adderley Park Road opened in 1881 and was soon taking over £60 per week. This photograph is of the new Branch No. 1 at Alum Rock Road and was taken in 1900. (As a shop moved to larger premises, it retained the Branch number, which can make research somewhat confusing!).

Right: Branch No. 2 opened a year later, in 1882, at the corner of 104 Coventry Road and Herbert Road, Small Heath. This picture shows a later Branch No. 2 at 311 Coventry Road, in around 1900.

The first Branch No. 3 opened in Cheetham Street, Nechells in 1882. This charming photograph is of a later Branch No. 3 at 363 Nechells Park Road. It is said that coffee beans were trampled underfoot here, so that customers would be tempted by the mouth-watering aroma!

Above: The Society's fourth Branch opened in 1883 in Ellen Street, Brookfields. By 1900, Branch No. 4 was located on the corner of Lodge Road and Heaton Street (on 'the Flat'); a later purpose-built shop (still Branch No. 4!) is shown here at 92 Hockley Hill.

Left: Branch No. 5 stood in either Park Lane or High Street, Aston (the information available is not clear) and is one of the early branches about which very little is known. It is thought to have opened in 1887.

Opposite: An even later Branch No. 3, now at 59-60 Nechells Park Road, photographed in 1905 and showing a wonderful window display of Christmas goods.

Above: Branch No. 10, Orphanage Road, Erdington, photographed in the early 1900s, was a magnificent store where you could buy all you needed, from mangles and 'oil–cloth' to shoes and sauce. Why shop in the city centre?

Opposite above: Branch No. 8, Stratford Road, Sparkhill was photographed during November 1941 in wartime guise. The word 'Birmingham' has been painted out to confuse the enemy should they invade!

Opposite below: Branch No. 10 High Street, Erdington first opened in 1900 in response to a request from local residents. This superb photograph cannot be positively identified – it could be of that store or a later one. Further branches in Erdington soon followed (still numbered 10).

Branch No. 19, 264-272 Dudley Road, Winson Green was an imposing department store with very decorative brickwork and distinctive lighting. The street furniture is equally interesting, the sign on the lamp-post reading 'Stephenson Place 2 Miles'. This view is from around 1910.

Branch No. 21, 775 Stratford Road, Springfield in 1912. It was was a charming little shop with mosaic decoration in the doorstep and beautiful stained glass. The packed windows carry a variety of eye-catching humorous posters.

two

The Move to
High Street

Although properties in High Street had been purchased by 1913, the outbreak of war in 1914 delayed construction of the new Central Premises, so it was in 1916 that 'this imposing building, five storeys high, was formally opened to the public with modest but appropriate celebrations'.

In May 1927, the Society acquired the Metropole Hotel (adjoining the Central Premises), which was used unaltered as a store extension for some years. It was eventually rebuilt and linked to the existing store by building under and over Scotland Passage.

An early summer sale in around 1926 and policemen need to control the queue emerging from Scotland Passage. In 1938, Carlton House, adjacent to the Bull Ring side of Central Premises, was purchased.

An air raid destroyed the Carlton House building in April 1941 together with those owned by the Co-op on the opposite side of the road. This wartime photograph shows the sites cleared and the windows boarded-up; the area opposite would become known as the 'Big Top' site as it was sometimes used for a travelling circus.

In 1951, the Co-operative Movement staged an exhibition at Bingley Hall, off Broad Street, to celebrate The Festival of Britain. Coincidentally, it was the seventieth anniversary of Birmingham Co-op. Here we see the store suitably decorated and a procession leaving for Bingley Hall.

This is how most Birmingham people remember the Co-op in High Street. On the pavement near the entrance to today's Pavilions Shopping Mall, there is a large rectangular manhole cover. Below this is an access point to the subway that once linked the Central Premises to the Big Top site.

The furniture showroom has on show a range of suites made by the CWS, also the manufacturer of the sewing machine on the far left.

A fashionable young woman tries on the latest style in the ladies' coat department on the second floor.

The interior of the Metropole Hotel premises while they were being used as a temporary store before the 1939 redevelopment.

Note the pneumatic cash tube on the counter of the Bespoke tailoring department.

Above: An evocative photograph, which shows children in the toy department, *c.* 1950.

Left: A publicity photograph for the electrical department.

Opposite above: The children's section of the Central Hairdressing Salon will bring back mixed memories for many people. The Triang pedal car is now a prized collector's item!

Opposite below: Men stand aside while the ladies search out a bargain in the men's shoe department.

The nursery department on the second floor in about 1960, where many an expectant mother bought her Restmor, Silver Cross or Co-op pram.

The Co-op often had problems with manufacturers; no one would supply them with radios or televisions, saying that the dividend gave an unfair advantage. The Co-op, therefore, decided to make their own and, to reflect this situation, they called the range 'Defiant'.

This view shows a diversity of stock in the haberdashery department on the ground floor, *c.* 1970.

The butchery counter at Central Food Hall, *c.* 1950. The butchery sold cooked meat, pork pies and a variety of other items manufactured at the Co-op Pork Factory, Vauxhall Road.

The familiar customers' checks, having been sorted, are now totalled to calculate dividend in the check office adding machine room, *c.* 1930.

The newly developed accounts department, photographed in around 1930, was responsible for many and varied financial activities including departmental accounts, insurance, wages, pensions and share contributions.

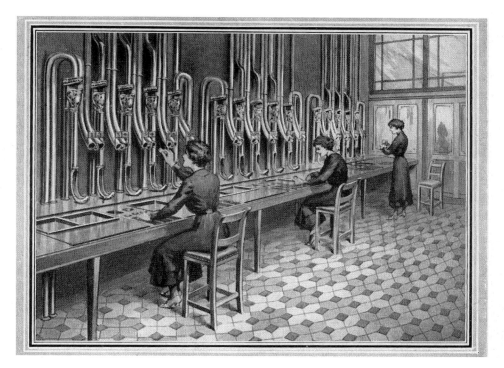

Most people fondly remember the pneumatic cash tubes. This drawing shows the Lamson Cash Office on the first floor in 1916. All the business floors had pneumatic communication tubes and the cash from twenty-two different stations was handled in this office.

Comptometer operators at work in the check office, Central Premises, May 1935. Ledgers and checks were kept secure overnight in safes, seen at the back of the office.

Above: This imposing photograph, taken in 1951, shows from left to right: Mr Green, vice-president in 1922, Mr Millington, president in 1922, Mr Ravenhill, president for over fifteen years and, on the wall, a picture of shareholder number one, the first president, Mr Roberts.

Opposite above: The president, Mr Ravenhill, chairs a meeting in the imposing boardroom in 1950. The contents were sold at auction in 1977 and a modern boardroom was created on the sixth floor.

Opposite below: The surviving officials of 1881 are pictured here in 1931. From left to right, standing: Mr C. Henman, Mr R. Holtham. Seated: Mr C.T. Beach, Mr A.J. Rigby, Mr G. Diddams.

Above: In 1926, the Society purchased the site in High Street known as the Grand Louvre, opposite the Central Premises. Almost all of the drapery department and some furnishings were transferred, with two floors being used for offices.

Opposite above: This wonderful view of the Grand Louvre, dated 1931, has been photographed from the Central Premises.

Opposite below: In 1928, the Midland Arcade was purchased for investment and expansion. This comprised seven shops with frontages on New Street and fourteen shops in the Arcade. The photograph shows the chemist's and optician's premises, Midland Arcade.

Above: The air raid of April 1941 severely damaged the whole of the Midland Arcade and Grand Louvre sites. Staff arrived at work to find their sodden stock lying amongst the debris.

Opposite above: Hats were de rigueur when this charming picture of the millinery department in the Grand Louvre was taken.

Opposite below: A comprehensive range of goods was offered in the hardware department. The 'Federation' bicycle is priced at £6-5-0 (£6.25), whilst a 'tea table for the garden' is only 3s6d (17.5p).

A completely new block of shops and arcades was built on the 'Big Top' site, opening in 1959 and advertised as 'The Society's Centre for Modern Living'. The third floor housed the popular 'Rainbow Suite', used for social gatherings, dances and theatre performances.

This last photograph brings to a close the High Street Chapter and shows the 'Record Rendezvous' on the ground floor in around 1960. This was a 'fab' place for teenagers to hear the latest hit records in specially insulated listening booths.

three

Celebrations

ENTRANCE for
TICKET HOLDERS ONLY

FD
4490

The Co-op was always keen to celebrate any anniversary or national event with exhibitions, concerts and parades. Here, onlookers enjoy a parade of horse-drawn floats winding its way along Paradise Street in 1921.

On Wednesday 2 September 1931, BCS celebrated its Golden Jubilee. Here can be seen a parade of decorated horses and vehicles, making its way along Bristol Street.

This float, from the Jubilee Parade in Great Brook Street, is carrying a 'Topper' folding wringer, which is one of twenty different models that were being made by the Co-op at the time!

Horses and wagons were loaned to other departments for parades; great pride was taken in the presentation of the horses, as this 1951 photograph shows.

Onlookers are urged to 'Join the Co-op' and to 'Eat Co-op Fruit' on this extravagantly decorated, solid-tyred Dennis lorry from the greengrocery department, May Day parade 1927.

A laundry department float, attended by a rather masculine 'woman' (that bizarre Co-op sense of humour at work!) poses for the camera in 1934.

A group of serious-looking children depicts famous nursery rhymes and fairy tales on this 1921 parade float.

International Co-operators' Day is observed on the first Saturday in July. This 1948 tableau celebrates 104 years of Co-operation.

In June 1933, the sixty-fifth Annual Co-operative Congress was held in Central Hall, Corporation Street, with an associated exhibition at Bingley Hall, the entrance to which we see here.

The president of the BCS, Mr Millington, poses for the official photograph prior to the opening of the exhibition, together with his committees and the orchestra.

'Congress House' and garden were built by the Co-op works department and formed one of the main features of the exhibition.

We are urged to 'Celebrate a great event – take home a Congress cake 1s worth 1s 6d' on the BCS Bakery and Confectionery stand.

A rare view of King Alfred's Place showing visitors queuing on a wet day in 1931, near the entrance to Bingley Hall, for the Golden Jubilee Exhibition.

'Empire' bacon was 1s (5p) per pound on the grocery department stand. The smartly dressed staff eagerly await the first customers.

A re-creation of the first BICS shop with a queue of boys presumably applying for the job advertised on the window (boys were expected to wear short trousers until their early teens).

Fashion displays were held regularly at the Jubilee exhibition, an opportunity to show what was available at Central Premises.

A replica self-service grocery shop was erected by the BCS works department at this Ideal Homes Exhibition, Bingley Hall. With the new method of shopping, suitable slogans were introduced such as 'Select the goods you think most suitable', 'The modern way of shopping' and 'All our stocks to choose from'.

The house built for the 1955 Ideal Homes Exhibition was furnished by the BCS. The electric cooker is for sale at £39/18/0d (£39.90) and the GEC washing machine at £81/6/4d (£81.32). The average wage in 1955 was between £7 and £8 per week.

Most people love to watch demonstrations and, in 1951, this machine was making potato crisps – the first time anything like this had been witnessed by the public. An added bonus was that, for 4d (2p), they could buy a packet to take home.

Another interesting demonstration, this time of an Aluminium Spinning Process to make basins, which were then sold to the visitors at this 1948 exhibition.

Father Christmas approaches Central Premises in High Street, *c.* 1950. His annual arrival was a major attraction in Birmingham and enthusiastic crowds would line the route into town to catch a glimpse of the procession.

Police are controlling traffic in this post-war photograph taken in High Street. Work is beginning on the new Co-op buildings behind the steel fence.

The children are wearing 'Drink Co-op milk every day' hats as they wait to see Father Christmas at the dairy department children's Christmas party in December 1947.

A rather forlorn Father Christmas sits by a wonderful array of pedal cars, prams, tricycles and dolls' houses (who remembers Mobo horses?).

The CWS invited the late Sir Stanley Matthews to help design football boots and a unique partnership began, which was to last for over fifteen years. Here, the publicity department has organised a visit by Sir Stanley and boys are queuing for their hero's autograph.

This decorated casket cake was made in the confectionery department to be presented to Birmingham City Football Club for reaching the FA Cup Final in 1956. Certain victory was anticipated, so a replica marzipan FA Cup was placed on top of the cake. When the team lost, a City Coat of Arms was substituted.

four

Suburban
Branches

Branch No. 100, Fox Hollies Road, Acocks Green opened in 1929. Despite the rain, many hundreds of people inspected the new shops at the opening ceremony.

Branch No. 49, Yardley Road, Acocks Green shows three distinct styles of lettering in the signs above the shops. The centre one is the earliest and probably the best remembered.

Branch No. 87, 181–185 Witton Road, Aston was a typical purpose-built group of shops showing butchery, grocery and, more unusually, a dry-cleaners which had replaced a confectionery shop. This was pictured in around 1970.

Branch No. 26, Corner of Balsall Heath Road and Upper Cox Street; Balsall Heath has an inviting display of fruit and vegetables which directs the eye to the splendid adverts on the walls. The arched entrance on the far left leads to the meeting rooms above the shops.

Branch No. 127, 321 Chester Road, Castle Bromwich in the 1950s displays a large sign in the window informing customers that the shop will soon be closing and a new self-service store opening nearby. Traditional prams feature prominently in many of these photographs, when women had to shop daily at local stores.

Branch No. 6, 7 Reed Square, Castle Vale opened on Tuesday 19 May 1970 in this newly developed area and the first day's takings totalled £1,016. Note the somewhat bleak surroundings.

Branch No. 10, High Street, Erdington was built with traditional materials combined with modern 'Staybrite' steel in this Art–Deco-style emporium. It was built and equipped throughout by the Society's works department and opened in 1936. Today, it is the site of a Midlands Co-op Superstore.

Branch No. 124, 728-730 Aldridge Road, Great Barr was a typical suburban shop. Mothers with children and prams were lined up for the camera but what were the men on the scaffolding doing? The building is now used by a tyre sales company but the BCS logo can still be seen.

Branch No. 54, 491 Bearwood Road was operated by a subsidiary company, Birmingham Co-operative Chemists Ltd, which had shops in various parts of the city. There was a shortage of pharmacists in chemist shops after the Second World War, as they left for employment in hospitals where there was no Saturday working.

A hardware department in an unidentified suburban store, possibly taken for an advertising or promotional campaign.

Branch No. 8, 381 Stratford Road, Sparkhill after modernisation, when the old system of storage boxes in the men's department was replaced by glass-fronted quick-service trays. This was around 1950.

Branch No. 8, 386 Stratford Road, Sparkhill, where the drapery department has undergone similar modernisation.

Branch No. 111, Walsall Road, Great Barr, which was later extended and is now an impressive parade of shops including a chemist, travel agent, funeral home, non-food store and supermarket, all owned by the Co-op.

Branch No. 103, 1494-1502 Stratford Road, Hall Green is a splendid run of shops (now occupied by various businesses) close to Robin Hood Island. Many of the larger branches had meeting rooms or halls above them, which would be used for Guild meetings, Co-op social events and could be hired for wedding receptions.

Branch No. 17, 279 High Street Harborne is pictured during the Second World War. The photograph can be dated by the car parked outside, which is edged in white to show-up in the blackout. Clues such as this are sometimes the only way in which probable dates may be determined.

Branch No. 13, 1066–1068 Coventry Road, Hay Mills nicely illustrates a typical conversion of houses to shops. Of particular note is the opening window and attractive tiling on the butcher's shop. There was also a CWS cabinet makers in Redhill Road, Hay Mills, where such diverse items as pianos and coffins were made.

Branch No. 106, 673-679 Kingstanding Road, Kingstanding was unique in having the largest self-supporting roof in Birmingham. The lack of interior support pillars allowed the shop fitters to position the counters in the best place for self-service. This impressive building continues as a Co-op supermarket.

Branch No. 125, Kitts Green was a prefabricated structure, ultimately to be replaced by a large supermarket nearby. This delightful photograph shows staff assembled outside their shop and illustrates the large workforce considered necessary at the time.

Branch No. 9, 204–206 St Vincent Street, Ladywood replaced an earlier Branch on Monument Road.

Branch No. 81, 107-111 Witton Lodge Road, Perry Common is seen here photographed in around 1970. The centre shop has been modernised as a self-service store with strip lighting and a new doorway, as it was realised that a deep doorstep wasted valuable selling space.

Branch No. 105, Cregoe Street, Lee Bank, 27 September 1948, an early example of a self-service store. Rationing is obviously still in force as the customer on the far right is clutching her ration book and there is a display of 'Points Goods' behind her.

An unidentified confectionery section which has been decorated for the Coronation of Elizabeth II in 1953; many of the items shown were specially produced for the occasion and carry her portrait.

This unidentified store is hosting a fish and vegetable demonstration, *c.* 1950.

Branch No. 116, Coventry Road, Sheldon in about 1951 displays a tempting selection of mouth-watering fruit.

Branch No. 138, 268-276 Church Road, Sheldon, in the district known as 'The Radleys,' incorporated living accommodation above the shops, as did many post-war branches. This store became a Co-op 'Pricefighter' shop in the 1980s and is still a Co-op supermarket.

Branch No. 2, Coventry Road, Small Heath was one of many branches built after 1901 to replace shops in converted houses. This was to become an important building, with grocery, boots, tailoring and drapery on the ground floor and furnishings on the first floor. There was a large meeting hall with a seating capacity of 450 persons on the second floor.

Electricity had not yet been installed in the area, so a small generator supplied the power for electric lighting. Imagine the scene on a gloomy February day in 1902, when the store was officially opened by the president of the Society, Mr W. Roberts. The original store was added to many times: fish, fruit and grocery in the 1920s and, by 1930, a chemist's shop on the corner of Coventry Road and Watts Road. The hall on the second floor was used for meetings by Co-op Guilds and Groups. It is fondly remembered by many for the cinema, where various films were shown, interspersed with adverts and stories of Co-operation. During the air raids in late 1940, the building was badly damaged by incendiary bombs but, because of a mix-up in bookings, it was not being used that night, so mass casualties were thankfully avoided; the second floor had to be carefully demolished. This photograph, taken on 20 February 1941, shows some of the damage, although the signs on the boarded-up windows announce 'Business as usual'.

Branch No. 21, 846–852 Stratford Road, Springfield displays the new Co-op logo which was introduced nationally by Mr Thomas of the CWS in 1968. This was an attempt to present a unified image and a variation of this is used today.

Branch No. 95, Warwick Road, Tyseley displays two distinct techniques of lettering. The Co-op had a long association with Tyseley, where there was a large and very productive CWS works manufacturing motorcycles, bicycles, prams, children's toys and other metal goods. There was also a shoe repair factory at 833 Warwick Road, which is now the site of a Co-op Electrical Superstore.

Branch No. 26, 653-659 Washwood Heath Road, Ward End, the shop on the left being the first to open. Premises to the right were gradually acquired until, by the 1960s, there was a parade of eight shops selling grocery, greengrocery, butchery, confectionery, drapery, fashions, shoes and dry-cleaning. Today, part of it is occupied by a Co-op supermarket.

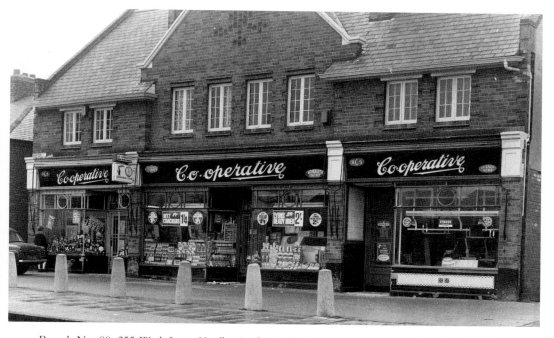

Branch No. 89, 255 Wash Lane, Yardley in about 1970 shows a run of shops, the like of which could once be found across most of Birmingham. Although many no longer exist, Midlands Co-op is once again opening new suburban branches.

The poster on the right in this well-stocked self-service store shows that the Society was celebrating its seventy-fifth anniversary in 1956.

The staff take a short break to pose for the camera in the butchery department of this unidentified suburban shop.

Pre-packed meat, introduced in the 1950s, would become the norm for many busy housewives.

Branch No. 115, Stoney Lane, Yardley is shown on dividend-paying day in April 1952. A temporary stall has been set up in the meeting room above the shop, presumably to encourage the housewives to spend their newly acquired 'divi'.

This Christmas
MAKE
SURE

MAKE THEM AND BAKE THEM WITH
Federation
Plain and Self-Raising Flour

The Co-op manufactured its own flour under the 'Federation' trade name. The quality and purity could thus be guaranteed.

five

Around the
Departments

The delivery of milk began in 1920, when heat-treated (pasteurised) milk was sold loose from the churn straight to the customer's own receptacle. This new dairy was built in Vauxhall Road, Nechells, in 1929.

The dairy was declared to be one of the finest in Europe. Milk was received in steel churns, which were then weighed and the contents smelled by a 'sniffer' to identify any sourness. Here we see sampling of incoming milk, in around 1940.

Milk of only the highest standard reached the customer and this photograph shows samples being checked for cream content and quality.

Bottled milk was introduced in 1923 and sold alongside 'loose' milk. The bottles were sealed with a waxed card disc and stacked in heavy wooden crates. Sterilised (long-lasting) milk was introduced in 1933.

This is an illustration of post-war mechanisation in the dairy department, Vauxhall Road on 7 May 1948. The mayor of Smethwick, Councillor A. Bradford, is at the wheel of a forklift truck while the mayoress (to the right of the truck), and other officials, look on.

Milk is still considered to be a near-perfect food and here, at the Tower Hill Welfare Clinic, mothers are encouraged to feed it to their children as part of the 'Beautiful Babies' advertising campaign in July 1947.

The thaw after the terrible winter of 1947 caused the river Tame to flood the road of its namesake. Co-op milkmen endeavoured to maintain essential supplies and the keen-eyed will spot the milk bottle in mid-flight!

Horse-drawn milk floats were withdrawn during the 1950s and were replaced by electrically powered vehicles, some of which are still in use. A Morrison-Electricar 25cwt D1 van is shown here.

Due to the importance of bread to working-class families, and to counteract the adulteration of flour, the Society was prompted to sell bread within days of opening. By 1884, bakery premises were obtained in Newdegate Street and, by 1908, a model bakery had been established in Great Brook Street.

The incorporation of the Soho Society in 1925 provided BCS with a much-needed bakery in Smethwick. New ovens were installed there and in Great Brook Street, giving the Society two of the best bakeries in the country.

The third, and largest, bakery was built in Manor Road, Stechford, in 1939. This photograph shows an automatic bread slicing and wrapping machine.

The wrapped bread is finally delivered to the customer's door by a cheery roundsman, as shown in this publicity photograph from about 1950.

It is not until 1902 that confectionery is mentioned in the Society's history, when a note is recorded of the 'purchase of half a dozen tins to bake our own cakes'. Here, the labour–intensive nature of the work is demonstrated by the three appropriately dressed young ladies. This was around 1950.

Parts of the bakeries were used for cake making until 1919, when a building in Adderley Road was purchased, the whole of which was eventually given over to confectionery production. Both photographs show staff at work in these premises.

During the 1950s, horses began to be withdrawn from service and, on 2 February 1957, the last horse-drawn van left Great Brook Street. Here we see one of the fondly remembered horses waiting patiently for the roundsman to return.

Electrically operated vehicles replaced horse-drawn vans and one of these Morrison-Electricar 20cwt D1 vans is now preserved at the Birmingham and Midland Museum of Transport, Wythall. A young baker's boy with an engaging smile stands proudly by his vehicle.

In 1891, the Co-op began selling coal themselves rather than through a local merchant. The opening of Acocks Green wharf in 1912 gave direct access by canal to the Cannock Chase coalfield. The familiar coalman and cart are about to set out from an unidentified depot.

Mechanisation allowed coal to be fed through a hopper directly into sacks on the back of this Austin lorry, ready for delivery.

This publicity photograph of 1949 displays the new Salter scales. Dr Beeching's closure of railway lines used by the coal trade contributed to the decline of coal usage, as did the introduction of 'Clean Air' regulations and the convenience of gas and electric heating. The fuel department closed in 1979.

An aerial view of the Birmingham Co-operative Laundry, which opened in 1931 at Holyhead Road, Handsworth. The impressive building is still there and is occupied by Sunlight Service Group.

Hard-working ladies are scrubbing by hand and using a dolly with a 'maiding-tub' in the flannel wash house of the laundry.

Somewhat less strenuous, but still time-consuming, work is being carried out in the hand ironing section.

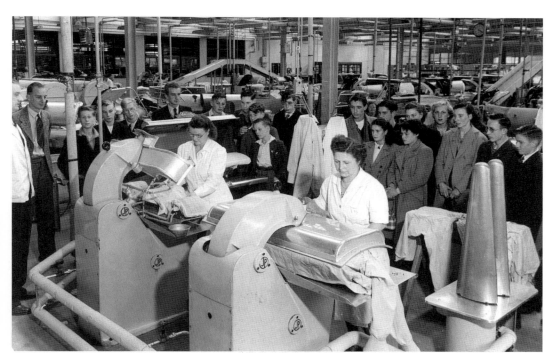

Members of one of the Society's junior training classes are being shown demonstrations of pressing at Acocks Green Laundry in 1950.

Above: Illustrated here is the trumatic sheet folding machine, which 'folds flat laundered work with mechanical speed and accuracy'.

Right: The garments are sorted, folded and finally wrapped, ready for delivery to the customer.

Opposite below: The laundry at Clay Lane, Yardley opened in 1939 but was soon requisitioned by the Rover Company for war work. It was returned to the Society in 1946 and continued as a laundry until the early 1970s, when business was transferred to Handsworth. The photograph was taken in 1948, showing the building still camouflaged.

Above: An obviously posed but nevertheless interesting photograph of horse-drawn laundry delivery vehicles. This was around 1930.

In 1919, the Society acquired Blackgreaves Farm, Lea Farm and later Woodhouse Farm, all at Lea Marston, nine miles from Birmingham. The photograph shows Lea Farm House in 1920.

Morton Paddox Farm was purchased in 1944, bringing the Society's total agricultural land to over 1,200 acres. For some time, the main building was used as a guesthouse for the Workers' Travel Association.

The land was used principally for milk production, cereal and potato crops. Potato pickers are busy at Lea Marston in February 1952.

This visit to a Lea Marston farm by the Woodcraft Folk gave city children the chance to experience the fresh air of the countryside.

The Birmingham Society began selling meat in 1905 and, from 1919, almost every new grocery branch had an adjacent butchery shop. Here, the president Mr Ravenhill and manager Mr Tuplin watch lecturer Mr Evans instructing a student in preparing meat.

The factory in Vauxhall Road started producing pre-packed meat when this became popular in the 1950s. Customers appreciated knowing exactly what they were buying and so drew confidence from seeing the details of price and weight on each pack.

six

After Hours
Activities

Football, cricket and bowls are still played regularly at the Co-op Sports Ground in Barrows Lane, Yardley, which was opened in 1923. These unidentified Co-op football teams date from 1931-32.

This successful 1948 bowls team from the accounts department comprised, from left to right, standing: W. Bloor and F. Beeson, and seated, A. Lamb, E. Williams, J. Glynn (captain) and T. Hodgin. In 1953, this same team (except for T. Hodgin) won the Interdepartmental League for the sixth time.

The Accounts Department Cricket Team won the Interdepartmental League in 1951. Pictured are, from left to right, standing: Messrs Griffin (umpire), Muddiman, Arnold, Duffin, Clarke, Reynolds, Fletcher, Stephenson (umpire) and seated: Fellows, Lewis, Penn, Horne and Lloyd. In the mid-1950s, a popular summer event was the Co-op's annual cricket match with Birmingham City Football Club.

There were few serious sporting opportunities for women co-operators, other than tennis and bowls, but in the liberated 1960s, a few daring youngsters formed women's football and cricket teams at Barrows Lane. This group of jolly lady bowlers is pictured here in about 1970.

A Co-operative Dramatic Society was founded in 1928, early performances taking place in the Belmont Room at Central Premises. This cast of *Annie Get Your Gun* is performing at the Rainbow Suite, in around 1965.

Amateur drama still flourishes at the Co-op in the form of The Midlands Co-operative Society Repertory Company, under the directorship of Sheila Palmer, seen here in the centre of the cast of *Lock Up Your Daughters* in about 1965.

A host of happy children of traffic department staff enjoy their party at Central Premises on Christmas Eve, 1949.

Musical evenings had been popular since the 1890s and a number of choirs existed by 1927, when the orchestra was formed. This Education Committee Concert Meeting took place in 1931 at the Town Hall and featured both the Society's choir and orchestra.

Jack Melling, a member of the Dyas Avenue Men's Guild and National Guild president, is shown here wearing the chain of office at the Men's Guild annual general meeting, Nottingham, 1956.

The links between the Co-operative movement and the Labour Party have always been strong. This electioneering meeting, at the Town Hall in 1968, was addressed by Harold Wilson and guests included Barbara Castle, Andrew Faulds, Dennis Howell and Frank Price. It was chaired by Mrs Mary Fynn (centre front), president of the Birmingham and District Co-operative Party.

From the beginning of the Co-operative movement, women had wanted to take a full part in its activities and not be simply customers. As a result, Women's Guilds were formed, the first Birmingham branch being started in 1900 by women from Duddeston and Saltley. The Kingsvale Women's Guild staged this tableau with an agricultural theme, in about 1950.

The main aims of the Guilds were to promote the Co-operative movement and to campaign for a better quality of life. By 1939, forty-four Branch Guilds existed in the Birmingham district, one of which, the Harborne Guild, is pictured holding a tea party in May 1950.

The Co-operative movement was instrumental in giving many working-class women the opportunity to broaden their education. It also allowed them to become involved in issues of concern such as health, divorce law reform and employment rights. These Guild delegates were attending the Congress at Central Hall in 1933.

Guild tableaux in parades and on gala days were not only fun ways of advertising Co-op products but also promoted the message that the Co-op gave value for money, as typified by the Ward End Guild, pictured here in around 1950.

The Yardley Guild joined the National Guild of Co-operators for this coach tour. This was around 1950.

Sparkhill Women's Guild is shown here celebrating its fiftieth anniversary in 1956. Today, only five Birmingham Branch Guilds exist – Fox Hollies, Hodge Hill, Northfield, Sheldon and West Boulevard.

Woodcraft folk are taught the art of potato peeling by leader Olive Palser, *c.* 1970. The Co-op is pleased to be associated with The Woodcraft Folk, an organisation with co-operative aims and principles, open to all children and young adults. They enjoy a varied programme including camping, games, craftwork, singing and dancing. The children are encouraged to work together, to be aware of the environment and to take an active part in the world around them. The movement is dedicated to the building of a more peaceful future, its motto being 'Span the World with Friendship'.

Unfortunately, only a few of these Woodcraft leaders can be identified: on the far left, wearing shorts is Mr Chapman, with Mrs Chapman on the right wearing the dark cardigan. The tallest man in the back row is Ted Palser. This photograph dates from about 1950.

In 1930, Birmingham Co-operative Society opened its own summer camp at Dunton Wood on its farm at Lea Marston. This group of Woodcraft Folk was gathered there in around 1950.

THE BIRMINGHAM INDUSTRIAL CO-OPERATIVE
SOCIETY'S EMPLOYEES

HAVE MUCH PLEASURE IN ANNOUNCING THAT THEIR FIRST ANNUAL

CONCERT & BALL

WILL BE HELD IN THE

DUDDESTON WARD HALL,

ON

TUESDAY, MARCH 8, 1898.

Mr. T. Bent's QUADRILLE BAND

WILL PLAY FOR DANCING.

M.C.: - - MR. F. HOLT.

The following Artistes have been engaged:

Mr. R. GARDNER, Mr. ANDREWS,
TENOR; COMIC;

Mr. W. RUDGE,
NEGRO ENTERTAINER;

Master E. ROWE, Master A. MARSTON,
SOLO VIOLIN; ACCOMPANIST.

REFRESHMENTS will be provided by MR. J. SIMPSON, The Junction Hotel, Bloomsbury Street.

DOORS OPEN AT 7.30.   DANCING AT 8.   CONCERT AT INTERVALS.

Tickets, One Shilling each,

May be had from MR. SIMPSON (The Junction Hotel), MR. F. HOLT, or from any of the Society's Shops.

A rare advert for an 1898 concert ball for the employees of the Birmingham Industrial Co-operative Society.

All Social, Industrial, and Political Progress is advanced by Co=operation.

Birmingham Industrial Co=operative Society, Ltd.
1 GT. FRANCIS ST.

The Annual

TEA PARTY, Concert, AND Soiree,

WILL BE HELD IN

THE TOWN HALL, BIRMINGHAM.

ON

MONDAY, JANUARY 17TH, 1898.

Tea on the Tables at 5 p.m.
Sandwiches Provided.

Chair to be taken at 7 o'clock by the President.
MR. WM. COPE.

An Address will be delivered by

GEORGE J. HOLYOAKE, ESQ.,
(Historian of Co=operation).

Vocal Music

WILL BE RENDERED BY

THE ABBEY QUARTETTE,
MR. T. CARTER (TENOR),
MR. T. W. CRUXTON (HUMORIST).

Refreshments will be provided by Mr. B. Rodway,
Horse Fair Restaurant.

MR. BIRD'S
QUADRILLE BAND
WILL PLAY FOR Dancing.

M.C.'s:
MR. F. HOLT,
MR. A. F. STOKES.

Dancing at 8·30 p.m.

Tickets: Inclusive, 1s 6d; after Tea, 1s.;
May be obtained from any of the Society's Shops, or from Members of the Committee.

Another Birmingham Co-operative Society poster, also from 1898, this one for a tea party, concert and soiree.

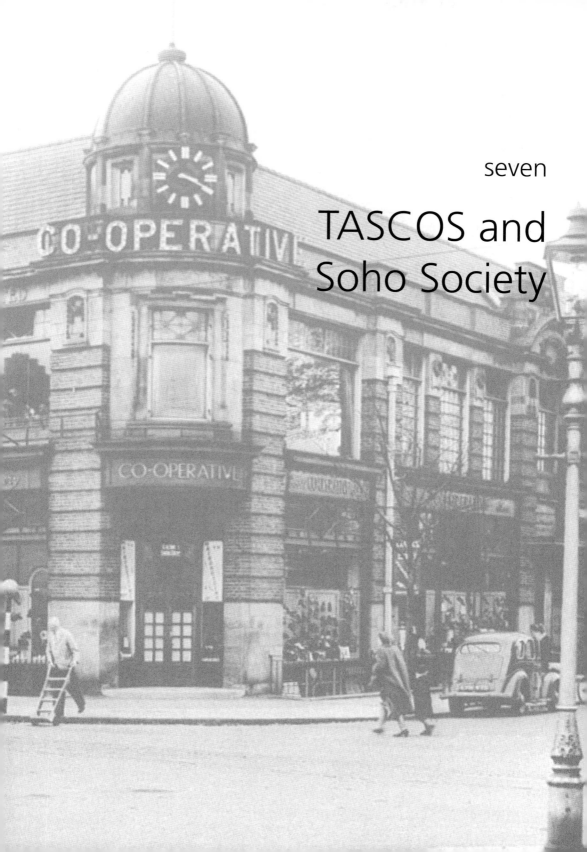

seven

TASCOS and
Soho Society

Tascos: Birmingham Co-op was preceded by the Ten Acres and Stirchley Street Co-operative Society, which opened its first shop in the front room of a house in Hazelwell Street, Stirchley in 1875. The founders are pictured in front of that house.

As trade increased, it was decided to build new premises in Stirchley Street (now Pershore Road) and these, complete with meeting rooms, opened in 1878. This is a view of the shop, now the site of a Midlands Co-op Funeral Home.

By 1914, the Society had twelve branches and had spread as far as Bromsgrove, absorbing the Aston Fields Society. It had its own dairy, bakery, coal wharf and education committee. New Central Premises were again needed, so this imposing building was opened in 1915 on the corner of Hazelwell Street and Umberslade Road (where the Co-op Superstore now stands).

A view along Hazelwell Street looking towards the site of the original 1875 shop. In the 1930s, the word 'Street' was dropped from the title, leaving the acronym TASCOS. In 1971 the Society merged with BCS.

Bread had been baked and sold by the Co-op in Stirchley since 1905; the 1950 history quotes, 'If the bread produced for a week was laid end to end, it would reach a distance of twelve miles'. This is the Central Confectionery shop at 1393 Pershore Road.

Branch No. 3, 768 Bristol Road South, Northfield opened in the early 1900s as a small grocery shop. In the 1960s it became a Co-op 'Superette' (small supermarket) and is now a Co-op non-food shop.

Branch No. 5, 295-299 Pershore Road South, Kings Norton was built to harmonise with the existing historical surroundings; this handsome building opened in 1936. There was a large hall on the first floor, which was used for various Co-op group meetings and was also available for hire. No longer a Co-op shop, the building still stands.

Branch No. 9, 476-478 Bristol Road, Selly Oak saw crowds of people and a procession of decorated vehicles attend its opening in 1908. Despite the optimism, this attractive shop did not fulfil expectations and became known as the Society's only 'white elephant'.

Branch No. 27, 143-147 Castle Square, Weoley Castle was a purpose-built shop which opened in 1932, one of the first shops in the area to serve the blossoming new estates nearby. For many years a TASCOS mobile shop was garaged at the rear.

Branch No. 41, 15-19 Alvechurch Road, West Heath has an interesting selection of everyday cars parked outside in this 1964 photograph, which are now considered classics. The shop is still a Co-op food store and provides a valuable service to the local community.

Branch No. 47, 44 Egghill Lane, Frankley Beeches was a modern self-service shop although deliveries were still made to customers by bicycle. TASCOS was always keen to open shops in developing areas and moved into this Council-built parade in the 1960s.

Branch No. 24, Alcester Road, Kings Heath features the grocery department staff of 1947-48. From left to right, Tom Tiernan, Bill Taylor, Frank Cotterill, Les Stokes, -?-, Jean Westwood, Dot Sandbrook and Barry Dale (who kindly supplied the photograph).

Soho: There had been Co-op societies in the Soho area since 1830, when employees of Boulton and Watt founded the Handsworth Economical Union and Provision Company. This group of fine upstanding men was the Soho Co-operative Society management committee of 1926.

The Soho Co-operative Society Limited was founded in 1887 by members of the West Smethwick Society, which had collapsed financially in the same year. History was repeated when, by the early 1920s, the Soho Society found itself in commercial difficulties. These are the Society's Central Premises in High Park Road, Smethwick.

The Society opened this grand building on Soho Road, Handsworth in 1920. After the merger with BCS in 1925, the new owners painted over 'SOHO' with 'B'HAM'. The 'SCS' initials above the shop were later changed to 'BCS'.

Birmingham Co-op constructed a single-storey extension on the side of the main building. It used amalgamation with the Soho Society as an opportunity to drop 'Industrial' from its title.

Stanley Matthews

SALUTES

THE VILLA !

Photo by courtesy of "Sports Argus"

Aston Villa F.C.—Cup Winners, 1957.

At Tascos Football Night

FRIDAY, SEPTEMBER 13th, 1957

At Stirchley Institute, Hazelwell Street, Stirchley

COMMENCING at 7-30 p.m.

★ **BRAINS TRUST ON FOOTBALL,**
comprising the whole of the Villa team, together with Mr. Eric Houghton (team manager), Mr. Jimmie Hogan (coach), and the greatest player of our generation—the one and only Stanley Matthews.

★ **PRESENTATION TO CUP WINNERS**
Mr. Matthews will present every member of the Villa Cup Winning Team with a pair of the famous football boots which bear his name.

★ **WIN A PAIR OF THESE FAMOUS BOOTS**
Members of the audience will also have a chance of winning a pair of these wonderful boots, as each entrance ticket will bear a number, and Mr. Matthews will make a draw during the course of the evening.

★ **HIGHLIGHTS OF THE LAST SIX CUP FINALS**
Relive those thrilling moments of the last six Cup Finals, including Villa's great victory of 1957, Birmingham City's fight against Manchester City in 1956, the Albion's victory over Preston in 1954, and " Stan's final " (Blackpool v Bolton Wanderers), of 1953.

Boys' Models from

21/-

according to size

ADMISSION 1/6 (Adults). 1/- (Children under 15)
Tickets can be obtained from Tascos Education Department, Hazelwell Lane, Stirchley, or from Tascos Footwear Departments at Stirchley, King's Heath, and Northfield. **Questions for submission to the players to be sent to this department by Wednesday, September 11th.**

In 1957, famous footballers were more accessible to the public, as this advert shows. The entire Aston Villa team and Stanley Matthews himself were guests at this football evening in Stirchley.

eight

Behind the
Scenes

When horses were requisitioned during the First World War, the BICS began using motor vehicles and the traffic department was formed to maintain them. This photograph shows 1930s delivery vans at Handsworth Laundry.

The mechanics are hard at work in the traffic department, Great Brook Street, *c.* 1930. The man on the far left, lying on his back, is Len Weston, who would complete almost fifty years service with the Society.

Hats were the order of the day on this charabanc outing in 1923. It must have been an uncomfortable ride on those solid tyres!

Birmingham Co-op organised excursions and holidays for many years, such as those at the Co-op Holiday Camp at Corton near Great Yarmouth. This particular coach, however, is taking part in a parade. This was the 1930s.

During the Second World War, Birmingham Co-op formed its own Fire Brigade; smartly uniformed members are pictured here outside the traffic department in May 1941.

During two air raids in one week, ninety-seven Co-op premises sustained damage, putting the Brigade under great pressure. On the wall of the traffic department, the word 'Birmingham' has been covered in case of enemy invasion.

An important aspect of transport was the Co-op Mobile Shop. They frequently served the post-war estates, which sometimes lacked normal shopping facilities. The arrival of the Mobile Shop was eagerly awaited by the residents and often became an occasion for socialising.

This Federation bicycle was made in the CWS factory in Tyseley and is featured here in the Birmingham Society's fortieth anniversary parade of 1921.

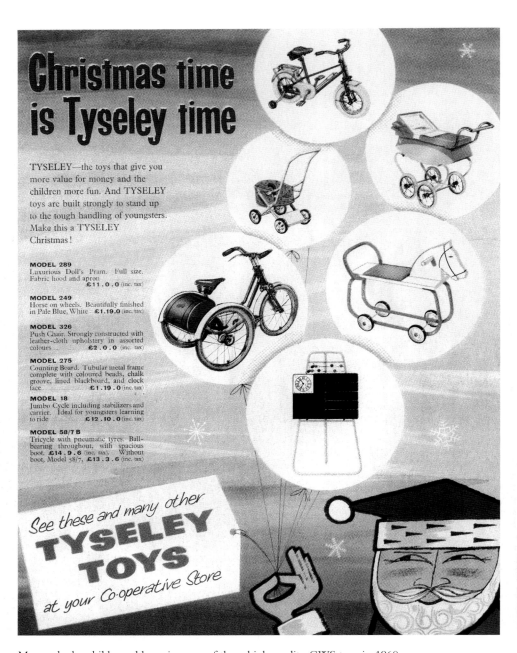

Christmas time is Tyseley time

TYSELEY—the toys that give you more value for money and the children more fun. And TYSELEY toys are built strongly to stand up to the tough handling of youngsters. Make this a TYSELEY Christmas!

MODEL 289
Luxurious Doll's Pram. Full size. Fabric hood and apron
£11 . 0 . 0 (inc. tax)

MODEL 249
Horse on wheels. Beautifully finished in Pale Blue, White **£1.19.0** (inc. tax)

MODEL 326
Push Chair. Strongly constructed with leather-cloth upholstery in assorted colours ... **£2 . 0 . 0** (inc. tax)

MODEL 275
Counting Board. Tubular metal frame complete with coloured beads, chalk groove, lined blackboard, and clock face **£1 . 19 . 0** (inc. tax)

MODEL 18
Jumbo Cycle including stabilizers and carrier. Ideal for youngsters learning to ride **£12 . 10 . 0** (inc. tax)

MODEL 58/7 B
Tricycle with pneumatic tyres. Ball-bearing throughout, with spacious boot. **£14 . 9 . 6** (inc. tax). Without boot, Model 58/7, **£13 . 3 . 6** (inc. tax)

See these and many other
TYSELEY TOYS
at your Co-operative Store

Many a lucky child would receive one of these high-quality CWS toys in 1960.

By 1950, the Society had eight hundred horses to draw its vast fleet of vehicles. This photograph and those on pages 120 and 121 were taken at the smithy and stables at Great Brook Street.

To attend to the needs of so many horses, twenty-five farriers were employed and their skill earned many certificates, trophies and medals, such as these won by Mr T. Smith in 1950.

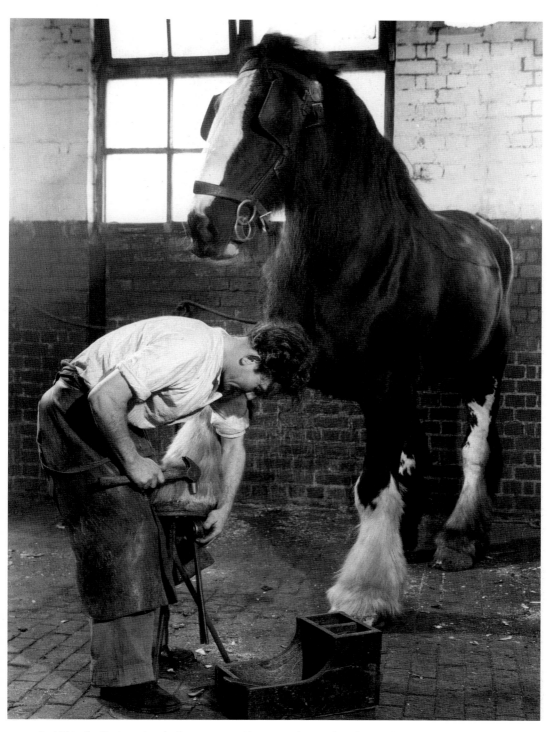

In 1951, the Society was the largest user of horses in the city but during the next decade, for reasons of economy and efficiency, they were gradually replaced by motorised transport.

These two interesting photographs of the Boot Repair Factory in Newdegate Street were taken in 1922.

In the inter-war years, shoes were relatively expensive so it was customary to have them repaired, rather than buy new ones.

An early scene from the cutting room of the tailoring department in Central Premises, High Street, which produced various uniforms in addition to the usual items of clothing.

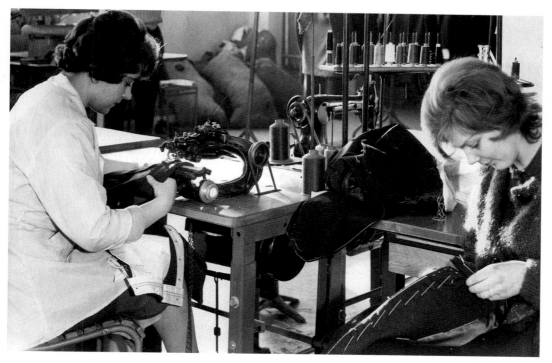

Two industrious young women are at work in the sewing section of the tailoring department, c. 1960.

This atmospheric 1920s photograph of the grocery warehouse in Adderley Road, Saltley shows flour being fed through hoppers into paper bags, the tops of which were then hand-folded.

Opposite above: This scene in a storage room of the grocery warehouse illustrates the large and varied amount of stock handled daily.

Opposite below: The Co-op liked to use catchy slogans such as the well-known 'Co-operative Tea is filling the Nation's teapot', seen here on cartons in the packing department. This was around 1960.

The Birmingham works department was formed in 1913 to carry out small repairs and maintenance. It was later also responsible for erecting and fitting-out complete shops, eventually employing over five hundred people. This photograph shows the joinery and shop fitting department at Woodcock Street.

The works department built most of the early important buildings, including the dairy, laundry and garages. The woodworking machine shop, shown here, was responsible for the handsome woodwork in the Central Premises boardroom.

The Birmingham Industrial Co-operative Society first provided funerals in the early 1900s using horse-drawn hearses. The enterprise was surprisingly short-lived given the nature of the business, but in 1935 the Society re-established the service, this time with far greater success.

The Birmingham Society's Funeral Service was the first in the city to use a fully motorised fleet of dedicated vehicles. The Co-op was justifiably said to care for its customers 'from the cradle to the grave'.